What Do We Know

Other Books by Mary Oliver

MARY OLIVER

What Do We Know

Poems and Prose Poems

DA CAPO PRESS
A MEMBER OF THE PERSEUS BOOKS GROUP

Designed by Melodie Wertelet/mwdesign
Set in 12 point Adobe Garamond

Cataloging-in-Publication data for this book is available
from the Library of Congress.

First Da Capo Press edition 2002
ISBN 0–306–81206–1
ISBN-13 978–0–306–81206–4

Published by Da Capo Press
A Member of the Perseus Books Group
http://www.dacapopress.com

Da Capo Press books are available at special discounts for bulk purchases in
the U.S. by corporations, institutions, and other organizations. For more in-
formation, please contact the Special Markets Department at the Perseus
Books Group, 11 Cambridge Center, Cambridge, MA 02142, or call (800)
255-1514 or (617) 252-5298, or e-mail j.mccrary@perseusbooks.com.

7 8 9

For
Molly Malone Cook

"The invisible and imponderable is the sole fact."

—Emerson, *Letters and Social Aims*

"My mind is on fire to understand this most intricate riddle."

— *The Confessions of St. Augustine*

Contents

What Do We Know

Leaving the house,
I went out to see

the frog, for example,
in her shining green skin;

and her eggs
like a slippery veil;

and her eyes
with their golden rims;

and the pond
with its risen lilies;

and its warmed shores
dotted with pink flowers;

and the long, windless afternoon;
and the white heron

like a dropped cloud,
taking one slow step

then standing awhile then taking
another, writing

her own soft-footed poem
through the still waters.

1.

Fat,
black, slick,
galloping in the pitch
of the waves, in the pearly

fields of the sea,
they leap toward us,
they rise, sparkling, and vanish, and rise sparkling,
they breathe little clouds of mist, they lift perpetual smiles,

they slap their tails on the waves, grandmothers and grandfathers
enjoying the old jokes,
they circle around us,
they swim with us—

2.

a hundred white-sided dolphins
on a summer day,
each one, as God himself
could not appear more acceptable

a hundred times,
in a body blue and black threading through
the sea foam,
and lifting himself up from the opened

tents of the waves on his fishtail,
to look
with the moon of his eye
into my heart,

3.

and find there
pure, sudden, steep, sharp, painful
gratitude
that falls —

I don't know — either
unbearable tons
or the pale, bearable hand
of salvation

on my neck,
lifting me
from the boat's plain plank seat
into the world's

4.

unspeakable kindness.
It is my sixty-third summer on earth
and, for a moment, I have almost vanished
into the body of the dolphin,

into the moon-eye of God,
into the white fan that lies at the bottom of the sea
with everything
that ever was, or ever will be,

supple, wild, rising on flank or fishtail —
singing or whistling or breathing damply through blowhole
at top of head. Then, in our little boat, the dolphins suddenly gone,
we sailed on through the brisk, cheerful day.

How wonderful! I speak of the soul and seven people rise from their chairs and leave the room, seven others lean forward to listen. I speak of the body, the spirit, the mockingbird, the hollyhock, leaves opening in the rain, music, faith, angels seen at dusk—and seven more people leave the room and are seen running down the road. Seven more stay where they are but make murmurous disruptive sounds. Another seven hang their heads, feigning disinterest though their hearts are open, their hope is high that they will hear the word even again. The word is already, for them, the song in the forest. They know already how everything is better—the dark trees less terrible, the ocean less hungry—when it comes forth, and looks around with its crisp and lovely eye, and begins to sing.

Always there is something worth saying
    about glory, about gratitude.
But I went walking a long time across the dunes
    and in all that time spoke not a single word,
nor wrote one down, nor even thought anything at all
    at the window of my heart.

Speechless the snowy tissue of clouds passed over, and more came,
    and speechless they passed also.
The beach plums hung on the hillsides, their branches
    heavy with blossoms; yet not one of them said a word.

And nothing there anyway knew, don't we know, what a word is,
    or could parse down from the general liquidity of feeling
to the spasm and bull's eye of the moment, or the logic,
    or the instance,
trimming the fingernails of happiness, entering the house
    of rhetoric.

And yet there was one there eloquent enough,
    all this time,
and not quietly but in a rhapsody of reply, though with
    an absence of reason, of querulous pestering. The mockingbird
was making of himself
    an orchestra, a choir, a dozen flutes,

a tambourine, an outpost of perfect and exact observation,
    all afternoon rapping and whistling
on the athlete's lung-ful of leafy air. You could not

imagine a steadier talker, hunched deep in the tree,
then floating forth decorative and boisterous and mirthful,
    all eye and fluttering feathers. You could not imagine
a sweeter prayer.

1.

When I went back to the sea
it wasn't waiting.
Neither had it gone away.
All its musics were safe and sound; the circling gulls
were still a commonplace, the fluted shells
rolled on the shore
more beautiful than money —
oh, yes, more beautiful than money!
the thick-necked seals
stood in the salted waves with their soft, untroubled faces
gazing shoreward —

oh bed of silk,
lie back now on your prairies of blackness your fields of sunlight
that I may look at you.

I am happy to be home.

2.

I do not want to be frisky, and theatrical.
I do not want to go forward in the parade of names.
I do not want to be diligent or necessary or in any way
    heavy.

From my mouth to God's ear, I swear it; I want only
    to be a song.

To wander around in the fields like a little reed bird.

To be a song.

3.

Two eggs rolled from the goose nest
    down to the water and halfway into the water.
What good is hoping?
I went there softly, and gathered them
and put them back into the nest

of the goose who bit me hard with her
    lovely black beak with the pink
        tongue-tip quivering,

and beat my arms with her
    lovely long wings
and beat my face with her
    lovely long wings,
what good is trying?
She hissed horribly, wanting me to be frightened.
I wasn't frightened.
I just knew it was over,
those cold white eggs would never hatch,

the birds would forget, soon, and go back
    to the light-soaked pond,
        what good is remembering?

But I wasn't frightened.

4.

Sometimes I really believe it, that I am going to
save my life

a little.

5.

When I found the seal pup alone on the far beach,
not sleeping but looking all around, I didn't
reason it out, for reason would have sent me away,
I just
went close but not too close, and lay down on the sand
with my back toward it, and
pretty soon it rolled over, and rolled over
until the length of its body lay along
the length of my body, and so we touched, and maybe
our breathing together was some kind of heavenly conversation
in God's delicate and magnifying language, the one
we don't dare speak out loud,
not yet.

6.

Rumi the poet was a scholar also.
But Shams, his friend, was an angel.
By which I don't mean anything patient or sweet.
When I read how he took Rumi's books and threw them
    into the duck pond,
I shouted for joy. Time to live now,
Shams meant.
                    I see him, turning away
casually toward the road, Rumi following, the books
    floating and sinking among the screeching ducks,

oh, beautiful book-eating pond!

7.

The country of the mockingbird is where I now want to be,
    thank you, yes.

The days when the snow-white swans might pass over the dunes
are the days I want to eat now, slowly and carefully
and with gratitude. Thank you.

The hours fresh and tidal are the hours I want to hold
    in the palm of my hand, thank you, yes.

Such grace, thank you!

The gate I want to open now is the one that leads into
    the flower-bed of my mind, thank you, yes.

Every day the slow, fresh wind, thank you, yes.

The wing, in the dark, that touches me.

Thank you.

Yes.

The flat rock in the center of the garden heats up every morning in the sun. Black snake coils himself there neatly. He has cousins who have teeth that spring up and down and are full of the sap of death, but what of that, so have we all. As for his sporting life, there are many things he can do and I have seen a few of them: he can climb a tree and dangle like a red-eyed rope out of its branches; he can swim; he can catch a mouse and swallow it like a soft stone. Also he can lie perfectly still and stare with his lidless eyes in the greatest hope: that you will not notice him. If you do, however, he will lift his chin and extrude the fray of his tongue, which many find frightening. But tell me, if you would praise the world, what is it you would leave out? Besides, he is only hoping that you will let him live his life.

And now that you have seen him, he looks shyly at nothing and streams away into the grass, his long body swaying like a suddenly visible song.

Beauty

When the owl
on her plush and soundless wings
rises
from the black waves

of the oak leaves,
or floats
out of the needles
of the pines

that are moaning,
that are tossing,
I think:
o she is beautiful

with her eyes
like burning moons,
with her feet
like twisted braids

of old gold
flexing and curling—
and I am glad to see her—
some wild loyalty has me

to the root of the heart—
even when she ruffles down
into the field
and jabs like a mad thing

and it's hopeless,
it's also wonderful,
so I thank
whatever made her—

this beast of a bird
with her thick breast
and her shimmering wings—
whose nest, in the dark trees,

is trimmed with screams and bones—
whose beak
is the most terrible cup
I will ever enter.

The Hummingbird

It's morning, and again I am that lucky person who is in it.
And again it is spring,
and there are the apple trees,
and the hummingbird in its branches.
On the green wheel of his wings
he hurries from blossom to blossom,
which is his work, that he might live.

He is a gatherer of the fine honey of promise,
and truly I go in envy
of the ruby fire at his throat,
and his accurate, quick tongue,
and his single-mindedness.

Meanwhile the knives of ambition are stirring
down there in the darkness behind my eyes,
and I should go inside now to my desk and my pages.
But still I stand under the trees, happy and desolate,
wanting for myself such a satisfying coat
and brilliant work.

The white stones were mountains, then they went traveling.
The pink stones also were part of a mountain before
the glacier's tongue gathered them up.
Now they lie resting under the waves.
The green stones are lovelier than the blue stones, I thought
    for a little while,
then I changed my mind.
Stones born of the sediments tell what ooze floated down
    the outwash once.
Stones born of the fire have red stars inside their bodies,
    and seams of white quartz.
Also I admire the heft, and the circularities
as they lie without wrists or ankles just under the water.
Also I imagine how they lie quietly all night
under the moon and whatever passes overhead—say, the floating
    lily of the night-heron.
It is apparent also how they lie relaxed under the sun's
    golden ladders.
Each one is a slow-wheeler.
Each one is a tiny church, locked up tight.
Each one is perfect—but none of them is ready quite yet
to come to the garden, to raise corn
or the bulb of the iris.
If I lived inland I would want to take one or two home with me
just to look at in that long life of dust and grass,
but I hope I wouldn't.
I hope I wouldn't take even one like a seed from the sunflower's face,
like an ant's white egg from the warm nursery under the hill.
I hope I would leave them, in the perfect balance of things,
in the clear body of the sea.

Raven with Crows

I was just
driving down-hill, in the early morning, when
surprise winged up from the road:
it was

Raven. This is
not a big bird, you understand, but an
impossibly big bird, its
chunky, almost blooming black beak

and its large unquenchable eyes
shine
like a small unheard explosion; it is
no crow, no perky, stiff-winged, head-bobbing

corn-meddler. Over it,
in a tree beside the road,
a dozen such crows gave great complaint,
and if you were a black prince

and lived
in the solitary mountains, and had
just come down
for a look at the village, and the villagers

all milled around you, storming and screaming,
you, too, probably, would be at your best:
silent, gleaming, not threatening but
beautifully acrobatic,

with an almost jointless ease
opening your heavy wings over
their bobbing, worried bodies, or falling
hawk-wise down air, then scooping

gracefully away,
not showing off, yet clearly
an advertisement for the more
than ordinary life, for the

remembrance
of the gorgeous and the powerful and the improbable. And then
it flew off, opening up as it went, to a hugeness unimagined,
the morning sky.

The pond is not a temple. The blue heron and the green heron are not the attendants of a temple yard. One of them, in fact, appears to be asleep. The yellow eyes at this moment are looking at nothing, and the little fish in their rainbow shirts are gliding peacefully by. There is an old story, often told, of a warrior frightened before battle, not so much for his own peril but for the strife to come, and the awful taking of life by his own sword. Suddenly a figure appears beside him — it is one of the gods, in the dress of battle and on his face an expression of willingness and ferocity. His speech is brief, and all-encouraging. Now the green heron, that looks like nothing so much as a polished jar waiting for flowers, shifts its body, stretching the dark maroon neck, the wild crown, the yellow legs. And now the blue heron is walking rapidly, one might say devotedly, along the shore. And the water opens willingly for the terrible feet. And the narrow face, the powerful beak, plunge down.

I am tired of explanations. Unless they are spoken by the best mouths. Black bear coming up from sleep, growling her happiness. Nighthawks snapping their way through the dusk. Or the voice of the wind itself, flailing out of any and every quarter of the sky.

Especially in summer. Especially in the fields, close to the ground. Listen! Let the high branches go on with their opera, it's the song of the fields I wait for, when the sky turns orange and the wind arrives, waving his thousand arms. Or, autumn! I hurry out to the middle of the field and stand where the tough goldenrod, seeded and tasseled, is vigorously tossing—until something thankful rises from my own body. The goldenrod lashes back and forth, each stem on its knuckled foot. Yes! Yes! Yes! And then the dry earth begins to anticipate, and then I fall to my knees, and then the flowers cry out, and then the wind breaks open its silver countries of rain.

The Roses

All afternoon I have been walking over the dunes, hurrying from one thick raft of the wrinkled, salt roses to another, leaning down close to their dark or pale petals, red as blood or white as snow. And now I am beginning to breathe slowly and evenly— the way a hunted animal breathes, finally, when it has galloped, and galloped—when it is wrung dry, but, at last, is far away, so the panic begins to drain from the chest, from the wonderful legs, and the exhausted mind.

Oh sweetness pure and simple, may I join you?

I lie down next to them, on the sand. But to tell about what happens next, truly I need help.

Will somebody or something please start to sing?

You are standing at the edge of the woods
at twilight
when something begins
to sing, like a waterfall

pouring down
through the leaves. It is
the thrush.
And you are just

sinking down into your thoughts,
taking in
the sweetness of it—those chords,
those pursed twirls—when you hear

out of the same twilight
the wildest red outcry. It pitches itself
forward, it flails and scabs
all the surrounding space with such authority

you can't tell
whether it is crying out on the
scarp of victory, with its hooked foot
dabbed into some creature that now

with snapped spine
lies on the earth—or whether
it is such a struck body itself, saying
goodbye.

The thrush
is silent then, or perhaps
has flown away.
The dark grows darker.

The moon,
in its shining white blouse,
rises.
And whatever that wild cry was

it will always remain a mystery
you have to go home now and live with,
sometimes with the ease of music, and sometimes in silence,
for the rest of your life.

Sometimes I am victorious and even beautiful —
as when I go down to the pond in the half-light
and wade out into the black water,
where I unloop the taut lines from the willow stakes
    and bend to the weight
and lift the trap from the water — not slowly and carefully
    as in ordinary work, but hard and fast —

and open it,
and stare down and see the turtle's foot-wide mossy shell
and he sees me
    and he thrashes

and I gaze into his pink throat and haul him higher
and he hisses, his eyes shine
and the tongue wags in the gaping, beak-shaped mouth
and I shake him from the trap, his thick head flashing,

    and he swims away

and I close the trap with the heels of my boots, and fling it
into the bullbriar wracked and useless,

and the pink sun rises and sees me, by the black water,
smiling,
    washing my hands.

Lion's Mane

It is
the largest sea jelly in the world.
Rosy as sunset, blurry as spilled blood,

it lives
in the cold, clear, deep water,
its slick, five-foot-wide body-purse

like a drifting temple bell, decorated
with long streamers
flickering and searching

downward.
For all the liveliness of my mind,
I have to work to imagine

its life of gleaming and wandering,
its bulbous, slow, salt comfort —
its terror

when the winds unbuckle the blue
sheets of the waves. I don't know
if it sleeps. I know

there is a mouth somewhere
in the underside of the broad, almost
glowing pouch. And I know that it comes, sometimes,

to disaster —
here, for example, on this summer morning,
in the warm shallows,

it lies motionless, like a daughter of the sun
tossed down, with
no hope of rescue. It is

full of rips and tears,
its bright color drains
outward into the kingdom of shells,

sea worms, crabs, and the other
busy tribes. For fear
of its dozens of crumpled, needled streamers, we

don't move it, we only stare
at the almost watery
flat-tire body. But neither

are we casual. Its red skirt
is ruined, it has become
a terrifying death-gown! and still

what do we know about its unwitnessed
deep-sea life? "Goodbye, brightness,"
you say, and I reach down

and touch, just once, lightly,
the spilled, torn, rosy, chill body that is both
strange, and not strange.

Each one is a small life, but sometimes long, if its place in the universe is not found out. Like us, they have a heart and a stomach; they know hunger, and probably a little satisfaction too. Do not mock them for their gentleness, they have a muscle that loves being alive. They pull away from the light. They pull *down.* They hold themselves together. They refuse to open.

But sometimes they lose their place and are tumbled shoreward in a storm. Then they pant, they fill with sand, they have no choice but must open the smallest crack. Then the fire of the world touches them. Perhaps, on such days, they too begin the terrible effort of thinking, of wondering *who,* and *what,* and *why.* If they can bury themselves again in the sand they will. If not, they are sure to perish, though not quickly. They also have resources beyond the flesh; they also try very hard not to die.

So heavy
is the long-necked, long-bodied heron,
always it is a surprise
when her smoke-colored wings

open
and she turns
from the thick water,
from the black sticks

of the summer pond,
and slowly
rises into the air
and is gone.

Then, not for the first or the last time,
I take the deep breath
of happiness, and I think
how unlikely it is

that death is a hole in the ground,
how improbable
that ascension is not possible,
though everything seems so inert, so nailed

back into itself—
the muskrat and his lumpy lodge,
the turtle,
the fallen gate.

And especially it is wonderful
that the summers are long
and the ponds so dark and so many,
and therefore it isn't a miracle

but the common thing,
this decision,
this trailing of the long legs in the water,
this opening up of the heavy body

into a new life: see how the sudden
gray-blue sheets of her wings
strive toward the wind; see how the clasp of nothing
takes her in.

Every day
the sea
proves to be
collapsible —

it goes away
rolling and sighing
heavily
out of the long harbor

to the very horizon.
Barefoot,
we walk out
across that level dampness

until we are very far from shore —
far from our house,
or any house,
stepping upon the moist plain

that is all that is left of the
weight, the flurry, the flung salt,
the flash and the dancing
and the big voice of the sea.

What's real
is the real question,
addressed by us but never
by the happy, go-lucky gulls.

Later,
when the sea has returned
as clean and blue as ever,
and we are back home,

in our yards, on our porches,
how curious to remember ourselves
just looking around
that emptiness,

and how we felt sad
without feeling lost —
or, even, strange —
or, even, bereaved —

the way we stand, sometimes,
in death —
or think we do —
in our purest, wildest thoughts.

On Losing a House

1.

The bumble bees
know where their home is.
They have memorized
every stalk and leaf
of the field.
They fall from the air at
exactly
the right place,
they crawl
under the soft grasses,
they enter
the darkness
humming.

2.

Where will we go
with our table and chairs,
our bed,
our nine thousand books,
our TV, PC, VCR,
our cat
who is sixteen years old?
Where will we put down
our dishes and our blue carpets,
where will we put up
our rose-colored,
rice-paper
shades?

3.

We never saw
such a beautiful house,
though it dipped toward the sea,
though it shook and creaked,
though it said to the rain: come in!
and had a ghost—
at night she rattled the teacups
with her narrow hands,
then left the cupboard open—
and once she slipped—or maybe it wasn't a slip—
and called to our cat, who ran to the empty room.
We only smiled.
Unwise! Unwise!

4.

O, what is money?
O, never in our lives have we thought
about money.
O, we have only a little money.
O, now in our sleep
we dream of finding money.
But someone else
already has money.
Money, money, money.
Someone else
can sign the papers,
can turn the key.
O dark, O heavy, O mossy money.

5.

Amazing
how the rich
don't even
hesitate — up go the
sloping rooflines, out goes the
garden, down goes the crooked,
green tree, out goes the
old sink, and the little windows, and
there you have it — a house
like any other — and there goes
the ghost, and then another, they glide over
the water, away, waving and waving
their fog-colored hands.

6.

Don't tell us
how to love, don't tell us
how to grieve, or what
to grieve for, or how loss
shouldn't sit down like a gray
bundle of dust in the deepest
pockets of our energy, don't laugh at our belief
that money isn't
everything, don't tell us
how to behave in
anger, in longing, in loss, in home-
sickness, don't tell us,
dear friends.

7.

Goodbye, house.
Goodbye, sweet and beautiful house,
we shouted, and it shouted back,
goodbye to you, and lifted itself
down from the town, and set off
like a packet of clouds across
the harbor's blue ring,
the tossing bell, the sandy point — and turned
lightly, wordlessly,
into the keep of the wind
where it floats still —
where it plunges and rises still
on the black and dreamy sea.

Crows

In Japan, in Seattle, in Indonesia—there they were—
each one loud and hungry,
crossing a field, or sitting
above the traffic, or dropping

to the lawn of some temple to sun itself
or walk about on strong legs,
like a landlord. I think
they don't envy anyone or anything—

not the tiger, not the emperor,
not even the philosopher.
Why should they?
The wind is their friend, the least tree is home.

Nor is melody, they have discovered, necessary.
Nor have they delicate palates;
without hesitation they will eat
anything you can think of—

corn, mice, old hamburgers—
swallowing with such hollering and gusto
no one can tell whether it's a brag
or a prayer of deepest thanks. At sunrise, when I walk out,

I see them in trees, or on ledges of buildings,
as cheerful as saints, or thieves of the small job
who have been, one more night, successful—
and like all successes, it turns my thoughts to myself.

Should I have led a more simple life?
Have my ambitions been worthy?
Has the wind, for years, been talking to me as well?
Somewhere, among all my thoughts, there is a narrow path.

It's attractive, but who could follow it?
Slowly the full morning
draws over us its mysterious and lovely equation.
Then, in the branches poling from their dark center,

ever more flexible and bright,
sparks from the sun are bursting and melting on the birds' wings
as, indifferent and comfortable,
they lounge, they squabble in the vast, rose-colored light.

Last night
the rain
spoke to me
slowly, saying,

what joy
to come falling
out of the brisk cloud,
to be happy again

in a new way
on the earth!
That's what it said
as it dropped,

smelling of iron,
and vanished
like a dream of the ocean
into the branches

and the grass below.
Then it was over.
The sky cleared.
I was standing

under a tree.
The tree was a tree
with happy leaves,
and I was myself,

and there were stars in the sky
that were also themselves
at the moment,
at which moment

my right hand
was holding my left hand
which was holding the tree
which was filled with stars

and the soft rain —
imagine! imagine!
the long and wondrous journeys
still to be ours.

The Lark

And I have seen,
at dawn,
the lark
spin out of the long grass

and into the pink air—
its wings,
which are neither wide
nor overstrong,

fluttering—
the pectorals
ploughing and flashing
for nothing but altitude—

and the song
bursting
all the while
from the red throat.

And then he descends,
and is sorry.
His little head hangs,
and he pants for breath

for a few moments
among the hoops of the grass,
which are crisp and dry,
where most of his living is done—

and then something summons him again
and up he goes,
his shoulders working,
his whole body almost collapsing and floating

to the edges of the world.
We are reconciled, I think,
to too much.
Better to be a bird, like this one—

an ornament of the eternal.
As he came down once, to the nest of the grass,
"Squander the day, but save the soul,"
I heard him say.

Gratitude

What did you notice?

The dew-snail;
the low-flying sparrow;
the bat, on the wind, in the dark;
big-chested geese, in the V of sleekest performance;
the soft toad, patient in the hot sand;
the sweet-hungry ants;
the uproar of mice in the empty house;
the tin music of the cricket's body;
the blouse of the goldenrod.

What did you hear?

The thrush greeting the morning;
the little bluebirds in their hot box;
the salty talk of the wren,
then the deep cup of the hour of silence.

What did you admire?

The oaks, letting down their dark and hairy fruit;
the carrot, rising in its elongated waist;
the onion, sheet after sheet, curved inward to the
    pale green wand;
at the end of summer the brassy dust, the almost liquid
    beauty of the flowers;
then the ferns, scrawned black by the frost.

What astonished you?

The swallows making their dip and turn over the water.

What would you like to see again?

My dog: her energy and exuberance, her willingness,
    her language beyond all nimbleness of tongue, her
    recklessness, her loyalty, her sweetness, her
    strong legs, her curled black lip, her snap.

What was most tender?

Queen Anne's lace, with its parsnip root;
the everlasting in its bonnets of wool;
the kinks and turns of the tupelo's body;
the tall, blank banks of sand;
the clam, clamped down.

What was most wonderful?

The sea, and its wide shoulders;
the sea and its triangles;
the sea lying back on its long athlete's spine.

What did you think was happening?

The green breast of the hummingbird;
the eye of the pond;
the wet face of the lily;
the bright, puckered knee of the broken oak;
the red tulip of the fox's mouth;
the up-swing, the down-pour, the frayed sleeve
    of the first snow—

so the gods shake us from our sleep.

Oranges

Cut one, the lace of acid
rushes out, spills over your hands.
You lick them, manners don't come into it.
Orange—the first word you have heard that day—

enters your mind. Everybody then
does what he or she wants—breakfast is casual.
Slices, quarters, halves, or the whole hand
holding an orange ball like the morning sun

on a day of soft wind and no clouds
which it so often is. "Oh, I always
want to live like this,
flying up out of the furrows of sleep,

fresh from water and its sheer excitement,
felled as though by a miracle
at this first sharp taste of the day!"
You're shouting, but no one is surprised.

Here, there, everywhere on the earth
thousands are rising and shouting with you—
even those who are utterly silent, absorbed—
their mouths filled with such sweetness.

Now comes the white-striped, sharp-nosed digger of dampness
    in her black and oily coat.
All night in the moonlight she has been wandering
    the stony beach; now she steps
into the gardens and under the street lights
    like a flat cat.

Her eyes gleaming and her tail aloft, she is afraid
    of nothing—not dogs, not policemen who see her
and do not remove themselves from their cruisers, but sail on
    down the dark roads.

Everything is famous for something: the eagle for power,
    the fox for cunning.
This one we know for her temper and also her smell,
    which comes from the wicks of fire.
Yet once I watched and heard her, deep in the woods,
    humming to herself as she carried
leaves into her humble house, that was nothing
    but a scratched-out hole.

Take care you don't know anything in this world
    too quickly or easily. Everything
is also a mystery, and has its own secret aura in the moonlight,
    its private song.

            If you meet her
don't be afraid, just stand still.
And, while you let her stare you down,

notice how she stamps her pretty, little feet.
Notice how she shines.

Now are the rough things smooth, and the smooth things stand in flickering slats, facing the slow tarnish of sun-fall. Summer is over, or nearly. And therefore the green is not green anymore but yellow, beige, russet, rust; all the darknesses are beginning to settle in. And therefore why pray to permanence, why not pray to impermanence, to change, to—whatever comes next. Willingness is next to godliness. Once I watched a swallow playing with a feather, high in the blue air. The swallow wanted to fly and frolic; the feather just wanted to float. Many times the swallow dropped the feather, which drifted away, then went diving and careening after it. There are so many things to do in this world, and so many things to be done. Right now I'm glad to be agile and insistent. But, later! Then, I'll be happy to give up the quick burst, oh darling and important world, and just float away.

Look, it's spring. And last year's loose dust has turned into this soft willingness. The wind-flowers have come up trembling, slowly the brackens are up-lifting their curvaceous and pale bodies. The thrushes have come home, none less than filled with mystery, sorrow, happiness, music, ambition.

And I am walking out into all of this with nowhere to go and no task undertaken but to turn the pages of this beautiful world over and over, in the world of my mind.

* * *

Therefore, dark past,
I'm about to do it.
I'm about to forgive you

for everything.

Their Wings

In summer the bats
fly like dots and dashes
over the evening pond

on the darkness
of their wings.
But once, in the morning,

one of them lay on the road,
struggling,
so I carried it off into the woods and laid it

in a mossy place, in an old stump, where it died
heart-thumping and hissing,
in the slump of its wings,

in the huge enfeeblement of everything,
and in what dread I don't know,
and in what panic I don't know either.

In death
it was a mad architecture —
its joints were too many; it shed

all sound, all power — became
a little heap of stiffness
with a monkey face.

At dusk the others still
whirl through the air,
content

in the fist of their bodies.
And so I see
how steep the fall for everything—

what all become
past howl and breath—how the eyes fill
with an endless void,

and the tiny rose of the tongue
grows still,
and the leaves around

don't seem to notice or care,
but lean forward, like green wings,
upon the air.

Her Grave, Again

1.

Late summer, and once again the egrets have come back.
They stand in the marsh like white flowers.
Like flowers slowly flying, they cross over the dark water.

And the palavering wind
is walking
through the pines

talking and talking—

not necessarily softly.

2. (Luke)

I suppose by now
the delicate click beetles, the dark and robust bacteria,
have gone skipping in and out of her silent house: her
    heavy, relaxed bones.

For now she is God's dog.
(The deep electric kindness of her eyes.)

For now her life is over, who never once did wrong.
(And still, in the fields,
a bird with a ruby throat is thrusting
its tongue into
the sopped lip
of the lily.)

The death went into her
like lightning
in slow motion,
it mashed her knees,
it ruined the red glove of her heart.

(God puts two fingers into his mouth. Above the long beard,
the nose hooked like a thin moon, one eye like Venus
and the other like Mars. And he whistles. And we come.)

3. (Remembering)

Her hum.
Her sturdy legs.
Her white teeth.
Her heart-cage.
Her dew claws.
Her eyelashes.

4.

Fabre told a thousand stories,
each one as true
as he could make it.
He looked and looked.
I do that too, so can you.
The little jumping spider has green eyes,
and here is the lid of the eye —
and here is the hair along the lid of the eye,
it's amazing!
Now, try a bird.

Look, here is the head, the horn beak, the waffle of the tongue.
Look, here is the narrow chute of the throat, color of sunrise.
And here are the toes curled on the limb in the
 valley of leaves.
Do you see it!
And then the bird, unhurried, as though filled
with a fragrance to which it must make some reply, lifts
its small, soft head, and begins

to sing.

5. (Remembering)

Often
she steps down into my dream
for a visit,
she hovers
as in the old days
at my shoulder,
she sulks
until we run out together
into the world,
then she prances

through the bogs and over the dunes
then she gallops back to me
as in the old days
and leaps against me
her body

as in the old days
touching me
with the two wings of our lives,

6.

love
and terror.

7. *(Matins)*

Now we are awake
and now we are come together
and now we are thanking the Lord.

This is easy,
for the Lord is everywhere.

He is in the water and the air,
He is in the very walls.

He is around us and in us.
He is the floor on which we kneel.

We make our songs for him
as sweet as we can

for his goodness,
and, lo, he steps into the song

and out of it, having blessed it,
having recognized our intention,

having awakened us, who thought we were awake,
a second time,
having married us to the air and the water,

having lifted us in intensity,
having lowered us in beautiful amiability,

having given us
each other,
and the weeds, dogs, cities, boats, dreams
that are the world.

Now that I'm free to be myself, who am I?

Can't fly, can't run, and see how slowly I walk.

Well, I think, I can read books.

        "What's that you're doing?"
the green-headed fly shouts as it buzzes past.

I close the book.

Well, I can write down words, like these, softly.

"What's that you're doing?" whispers the wind, pausing
in a heap just outside the window.

Give me a little time, I say back to its staring, silver face.
It doesn't happen all of a sudden, you know.

"Doesn't it?" says the wind, and breaks open, releasing
distillation of blue iris.

And my heart panics not to be, as I long to be,
the empty, waiting, pure, speechless receptacle.

Walking to Oak-Head Pond, and Thinking of the Ponds
I Will Visit in the Next Days and Weeks

What is so utterly invisible
as tomorrow?
Not love,
not the wind,

not the inside of a stone.
Not anything.
And yet, how often I'm fooled —
I'm wading along

in the sunlight —
and I'm sure I can see the fields and the ponds shining
days ahead —
I can see the light spilling

like a shower of meteors
into next week's trees,
and I plan to be there soon —
and, so far, I am

just that lucky,
my legs splashing
over the edge of darkness,
my heart on fire.

I don't know where
such certainty comes from —
the brave flesh
or the theater of the mind —

but if I had to guess
I would say that only
what the soul is supposed to be
could send us forth

with such cheer
as even the leaf must wear
as it unfurls
its fragrant body, and shines

against the hard possibility of stoppage
which, day after day,
before such brisk, corpuscular belief,
shudders, and gives way.

Early Snow

Amazed I looked
out of the window and saw
the early snow coming down casually,
almost drifting, over

the gardens, then the gardens began
to vanish as each white, six-pointed
snowflake lay down without a sound with all
the others. I thought, how incredible

were their numbers. I thought of dried
leaves drifting spate after spate
out of the forests,
the fallen sparrows, the hairs of all our heads,

as, still, the snowflakes went on pouring softly through
what had become dusk or anyway flung
a veil over the sun. And I thought
how not one looks like another

though each is exquisite, fanciful, and
falls without argument. It was now nearly
evening. Some crows landed and tried
to walk around then flew off. They were perhaps

laughing in crow talk or anyway so it seemed
and I might have joined in, there was something
that wonderful and refreshing
about what was by then a confident, white blanket

carrying out its
cheerful work, covering ruts, softening
the earth's trials, but at the same time
there was some kind of almost sorrow that fell

over me. It was
the loneliness again. After all
what is Nature, it isn't
kindness, it isn't unkindness. And I turned

and opened the door, and still the snow poured down
smelling of iron and the pale, vast eternal, and
there it was, whether I was ready or not:
the silence; the blank, white, glittering sublime.

At twilight an angel was standing in the garden. It is true, the wings are very beautiful. Even more spectacular, in a quieter way, is the light that shines out of the angel's body. Not the cold light of the glow worm, but the softer light of a candle, or more exactly the light of a candle as it is seen through a window and, therefore, is not only itself but the light and a kind of veil together, which in fact does not double the mystery but multiplies it. The angel was looking into the trees, but mostly it was just standing there. In a strange and inexplicable way, it seemed as familiar to me as the trees themselves. I was glad it was there, but didn't expect more—I mean I didn't expect the angel to stir from its place anymore than I expected the trees to start walking around. The trees and the angel, they were each just what they were.

And yet, I am not quite telling the truth when I talk of such contentment. Once I woke in the night and was exasperated entirely, for an angel in those days, and nights too, had come into our house—had come that far—and hovered there. Why doesn't the angel help me, I thought, as I exhausted myself doing what had to be done. But the angel did not. It was, as I said, like a light behind a veil, as though Heaven's purpose could not trade itself for the business, even the grief, of the earth. Which is just one more mystery and, finally, the one I think about most. What, then, is their earnest business? What do the flames mean that spark from under their feet? Was I wrong, did the angel in the dark offer tenderness, and did I miss it? And what was that other angel doing in the garden, standing there straight-limbed and substantial, as though the trees were singing to him, or he was singing to the leaves, or all of them were stitching a music together for something or someone, and no time no precious time to think of anything else.

Snow Buntings

Nothing
all winter,
floats to our ears
more brightly

than the voices
of the sand-colored
snow buntings
that twirl from the north—

that come
tireless through the wind—
that graze
in the barest fields,

on the smallest seed,
that pour forth
their faint phrases
like flakes of water,

like bits of glaze
tapping against each other
calmly
in the white cave,

in the blue hair
of the storm.
How long is winter,
and how shall we bear it?

Day after day
they dip down
out of the clouds
and into the world

to chirr and spangle
among the rows
of corn root,
the silent snow,

until the earth is lifted
out of the great weight
of brokenness
by their clear voices

that shake
like beads of light
across the lonely fields, to make them
glow.

Years ago,
in the bottle-green light
of the cold January sea,

two seals
suddenly appeared together
in a single uplifting wave —

each in exactly the same relaxed position —
each, like a large, black comma,
upright and staring;

it was like a painting
done twice
and, twice, tenderly.

The wave hung, then it broke apart;
its lip was lightning;
its floor was the blow of sand

over which the seals rose and twirled and were gone.
Of all the reasons for gladness,
what could be foremost of this one,

that the mind can seize both the instant and the memory!
Now the seals are no more than the salt of the sea.
If they live, they're more distant than Greenland.

But here's the kingdom we call remembrance
with its thousand iron doors
through which I pass so easily,

switching on the old lights as I go—
while the dead wind rises and the old rapture rewinds,
the stiff waters once more begin to kick and flow.

I thought I heard them
in some vines
swinging down
in a yard

across the road,
so I went
this afternoon
across the white-sheeted fields,

slowly,
and listening hard,
until I found them
beside a shining creek

that was rattling
icily along—
they were foraging
the frozen buckberries

and calling out to each other
in delicate
wafers of sound.
The last time

I saw them
it was half the country away—
almost,
you might say,

in another world—
anyway, at a house
I no longer go to,
whose people

are all dead now,
whose graves, even,
I don't visit.
And the little birds

looked exactly the same!
Trim and bold,
and empty of any memory
that could break the spell

of the moment,
they flew from branch to branch;
they sang
in the great, white cold.

The Loon

Not quite four a.m., when the rapture of being alive
strikes me from sleep, and I rise
from the comfortable bed and go
to another room, where my books are lined up
in their neat and colorful rows. How

magical they are! I choose one
and open it. Soon
I have wandered in over the waves of the words
to the temple of thought.

            And then I hear
outside, over the actual waves, the small,
perfect voice of the loon. He is also awake,
and with his heavy head uplifted he calls out
to the fading moon, to the pink flush
swelling in the east that, soon,
will become the long, reasonable day.

                Inside the house
it is still dark, except for the pool of lamplight
in which I am sitting.

          I do not close the book.

Neither, for a long while, do I read on.

Last night, an owl
in the blue dark
tossed
an indeterminate number

of carefully shaped sounds into
the world, in which,
a quarter of a mile away, I happened
to be standing.

I couldn't tell
which one it was —
the barred or the great-horned
ship of the air —

it was that distant. But, anyway,
aren't there moments
that are better than knowing something,
and sweeter? Snow was falling,

so much like stars
filling the dark trees
that one could easily imagine
its reason for being was nothing more

than prettiness. I suppose
if this were someone else's story
they would have insisted on knowing
whatever is knowable — would have hurried

over the fields
to name it — the owl, I mean.
But it's mine, this poem of the night,
and I just stood there, listening and holding out

my hands to the soft glitter
falling through the air. I love this world,
but not for its answers.
And I wish good luck to the owl,

whatever its name —
and I wish great welcome to the snow,
whatever its severe and comfortless
and beautiful meaning.

A mink,
    jointless as heat, was
tip-toeing along
    the edge of the creek,

which was still in its coat of snow,
    yet singing—I could hear it!—
the old song
    of brightness.

It was one of those places,
    turning and twisty,
that Ruskin might have painted, though
    he didn't. And there were trees
leaning this way and that,
    seed-beaded

buckthorn mostly, but at the moment
    no bird, the only voice
that of the covered water—like a long,
    unknotted thread, it kept
slipping through. The mink
    had a hunger in him

bigger than his shadow, which was gathered
    like a sheet of darkness under his
neat feet which were busy
    making dents in the snow. He sniffed
slowly and thoroughly in all
    four directions, as though

it was a prayer to the whole world, as far
    as he could capture its beautiful
smells — the iron of the air, the blood
    of necessity. Maybe, for him, even
the pink sun fading away to the edge
    of the world had a smell,

of roses, or of terror, who knows
    what his keen nose was
finding out. For me, it was the gift of the winter
    to see him. Once, like a hot, dark-brown pillar,
he stood up — and then he ran forward, and was gone.
    I stood awhile and then walked on

over the white snow: the terrible, gleaming
    loneliness. It took me, I suppose,
something like six more weeks to reach
    finally a patch of green, I paused so often
to be glad, and grateful, and even then carefully across
    the vast, deep woods I kept looking back.

I thank the editors of the following magazines, in which, sometimes in a slightly different form, some of the poems in this volume were first published.

The American Scholar: Clam, The Loon

Appalachia: Raven with Crows, Wind

Cape Cod Voice: Blue Iris, The Roses

Cybernetics and Human Knowing: Summer Poem

DoubleTake: Black Snake, Mockingbird

Five Points: Heron Rises from the Dark, Summer Pond; Last Night the Rain Spoke to Me; Tree Sparrows; Walking to Oak-Head Pond, and Thinking of the Ponds I Will Visit in the Next Days and Weeks

Image: Moonlight, Snowy Night, Stones, The Word

Michigan Quarterly Review: On Losing a House

Shenandoah: Beauty, Oranges

The Southern Review: Sometimes I Am Victorious and Even Beautiful, Their Wings

Witness: Gratitude, Mink

Crows, Early Snow, One Hundred White-sided Dolphins on a Summer Day, and Winter at Herring Cove originally appeared in *The New Yorker.*